Contents

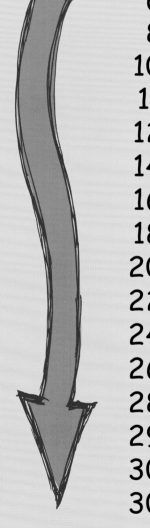

What's that noise?

What sounds can you hear?

Brrrrm!

Maybe you can hear the noise of a car.

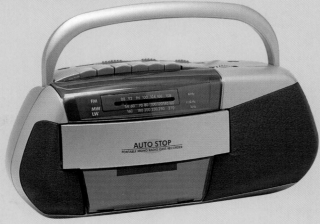

Or maybe you hear the sound of a radio.

Trevor hears three sounds. He can tell that the bird is above him.

Squawk!

Where are the other sounds coming from?

Toot!

Where are the sounds coming from around you?

Hello!

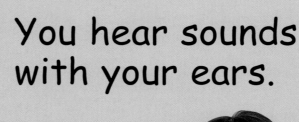

Ears

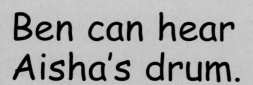

You hear sounds with your ears.

Ben can hear Aisha's drum.

He puts his hands over his ears to block out the noise.

Listen to a sound. Put your hands over your ears. How does the sound change?

Emma is whispering. Beth cups her hand around her ear to hear better.

Peter is deaf. He cannot hear sounds well. A hearing aid in his ear helps him hear sounds better.

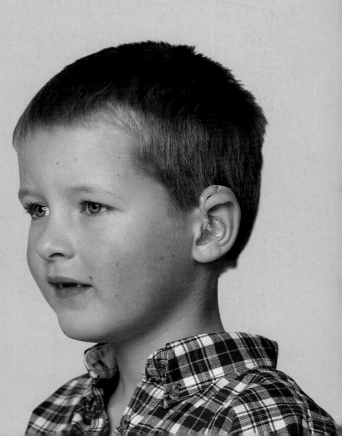

Loud sounds

Boom Boom Boom

A drum makes a loud sound.

A bus makes a loud sound.

Roar Roar

Roar Roar

What other things make loud sounds?

Purr Purr

A happy cat makes a quiet sound.

Leaves make a quiet sound.

Rustle

Rustle

What other things make quiet sounds?

Rustle

11

Listen!

Jo scrapes a
feather on paper.
It makes a quiet sound.

Peter wants
to hear the
sound better.
He moves
closer to Jo.

Aisha makes a loud sound when she shouts.

Ben does not like the noise. What does he do? Think about the answer then turn the page.

13

Near and far

Ben walks away from Aisha. Her shouts become quieter.

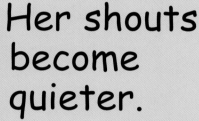

What will happen if Ben continues to move away from Aisha?

Stand close to a computer and listen to it humming. Walk away from it. How far must you go until you cannot hear it?

What do you do when the television is too quiet? Do you move closer to it? What else could you do?

High and low

Ping!

You make a high sound when you say 'ping'.

Miaow...

These are high sounds as well.

Ting!

Can you think of any more high sounds?

16

You make
a low sound
when you
say 'toe'.

Toe!

Grrrr...

These are low
sounds as well.

Phew!

Can you think
of any more
low sounds?

Long and short

Some sounds are long sounds.

Karen makes a long sound when she scrapes a bow across the violin strings.

Pull a fork across a plate to make a long scraping sound.

Some sounds are
short sounds.

Karen plucks a
string to make
a short sound.

Stretch
elastic bands
around a
box. Pluck
them to
make short
sounds.

Here are some musical instruments. They make different kinds of sounds.

What could you use to make a high sound?

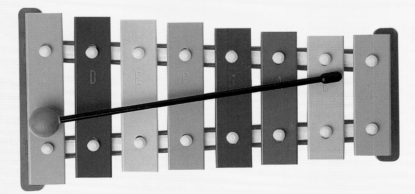

What could you use to make a low sound?

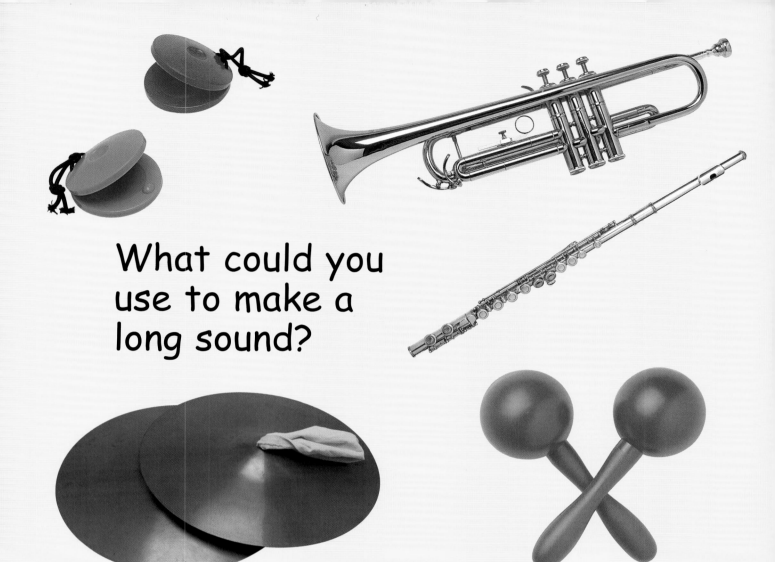

What could you
use to make a
long sound?

What could you
use to make a
short sound?

How do you make each instrument
sound? Find the answers to this
question on page 23.

Sorting **sounds**

You can sort instruments into groups by the way you make them sound.

You hit cymbals to make sound.

You shake maracas.

You blow a trumpet.

22

Here is a pictogram.
It shows the instruments from pages 20 and 21 sorted into groups.

What other instruments could you add to the pictogram? Make a copy and add your ideas.

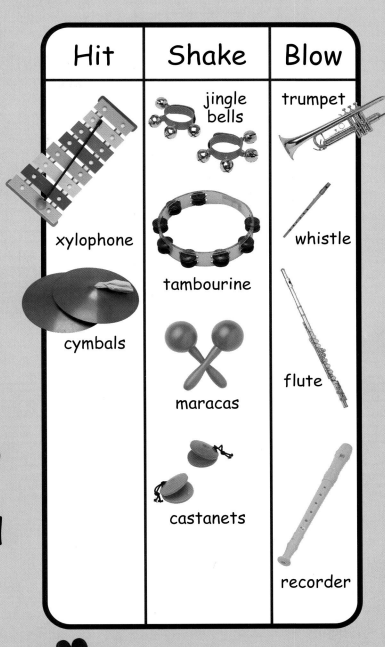

Hit	Shake	Blow
xylophone	jingle bells	trumpet
cymbals	tambourine	whistle
	maracas	flute
	castanets	recorder

Could you put a violin in your pictogram?

Make a  **shaker**

Tim is making a shaker.

1. He opens a tin.

2. He puts some rice in.

3. He shuts the lid.

4. He shakes the tin.

Make a rice shaker.
Make a shaker
with cotton wool, too.

Shake the tin
with rice in, then
shake the tin with
cotton wool in.

Which is louder and which is quieter?

Make two more shakers:
one with paper clips and
one with tissue paper.

Which of your four
shakers is the loudest?
Which is the quietest?

Body sounds

You can make many sounds with your body.

Sing

Slap

Laugh

Click

26

Stamp

Experiment
with each
of your
body sounds:

Clap

Whistle

Make loud sounds.
Find ways to make
them quieter.

Make high sounds.
Find ways to make
them low.

Now try it the
other way around.

Useful words

cymbals - an instrument made of two pieces of round metal that you play by hitting together.

ear - the part of your body you hear sounds with.

hearing aid - a simple machine which makes sounds louder. It helps deaf people hear better.

high - when a sound is squeaky. For example, a child's voice is high.

instrument - a tool used to make music.

loud - when a sound is very noisy and easy to hear.

low - when a sound is deep. For example, a man's voice is low.

maracas - an instrument containing beads that you play by shaking.

quiet - when a sound is very gentle and hard to hear.

trumpet - an instrument made of metal that you play by blowing.

violin - an instrument made of wood that you play by scraping a bow across the strings or plucking.

Some  answers

Here are some answers to the questions we have asked in this book. Don't worry if you had some different answers to ours; you may be right, too. Talk through your answers with other people and see if you can explain why they are right.

page 7	Trevor hears sounds from below right and left.
page 8	The sounds are quieter and less clear (muffled).
page 10	Here are just a few ideas of things that make loud sounds: aircraft, road drills, police sirens.
page 11	Here are just a few ideas of things that make quiet sounds: tip-toeing, breathing, buzzing insects.
page 14	If Ben moves a long way from Aisha, he will not be able to hear her shouting at all.
page 15	We can't tell you the answer to the computer question – measure the distance yourself to find out. To hear the TV better, you could turn up the volume!
page 16	Here are just some things that make high sounds: whistles, a baby crying, birds singing.
page 17	Here are just some things that make low sounds: a drum, thunder, waves hitting the beach.
pages 20-21	The best way to answer these questions is to try it out for yourself. Here's a hint: some instruments can make high, low, long and short sounds!
page 23	You would need to add another column to the pictogram to fit in the violin. It can be scraped with a bow, or it can be plucked (see pages 18 and 19).
page 25	Make the shakers and find out the answers yourself.

Index

About this book

Ways into Science is designed to encourage children to begin to think about their everyday world in a scientific way, examining cause and effect through close observation, recording results and discussing what they have seen. Here are some pointers to gain the maximum use from **Sound**.

• Working through this book will introduce the basic concepts of sound and also some of the language structures and vocabulary associated with it (for example comparatives such as loud and louder). This will prepare the child for more formal work on sound later in the school curriculum.

• On pages 13 and 21 children are invited to predict the results of a particular action. Ensure you discuss the reason for any answer they give in some depth before turning over the page. Remember, in most situations, our solution is only one of several possibilities. Set up other scenarios for the children to predict and discuss possible outcomes.

• You can use the book to introduce new ideas to the children. For example, the question at the end of page 15 points to a familiar but different way of making sounds louder on a TV – turning up the volume! And there are plenty of opportunities to begin to make the link between sound and movement.

• Discuss with them throughout the best way to record their results. The pictogram on page 23 is just one example.

• Ask them to make simple comparisons. For example, on page 25, do hard objects always make a louder sound in the shaker than soft ones?